Sugar Mice and Sticklebacks

Childhood Memories of a Hertfordshire Village Lad

Harry Edwards

The Book Castle

This book is dedicated to the memory of all the children of Hertingfordbury with whom I spent many happy years

First published June 1998
by
The Book Castle
12 Church Street
Dunstable
Bedfordshire LU5 4RU

ISBN 1 871199 88 3

Printed by Progressive Printing (UK) Ltd., Leigh-on-Sea, Essex.

Contents

1
The Village

HERTINGFORDBURY, where I was born and spent my childhood, lies in the valley of the River Mimram, a tributary of the River Lea, which in turn flows into the mighty Thames. A community of about one hundred and fifty inhabitants, the village is quiet now. The busy A414 which carried traffic through it on its way to the east coast now bypasses it to the north-east, across the fields and meadows where I played as a child. A large traffic roundabout marks the beginning of the bypass and an insignificant signpost points to Hertingfordbury. But to go back to how it was. . . .

Two miles from its parent town, Hertford, one entered the village where the main road was joined by the quaintly-named Thieves Lane, forming a triangle in which stood Dell Cottage, the home of Sir Henry and Lady Richards, gentlefolk in every sense of the word, with its well-tended lawns and dovecote filling in the delta. Sir Henry drove a beautiful green Daimler with pre-selected gears, and was one of the few car owners in the village. Beyond, on the left behind a high brick wall, was an eighteenth-century mansion called "Epcombs", the home of Mrs. Leslie, one of the wealthy ladies of the village, and a great benefactor, while on the right were the stables and kitchen gardens belonging to the house, leading on to Mr. Topham's farm and the river, which passed under the road at this point. Mr. Topham drove a bullnosed Morris, while Mrs. Leslie owned a large car which was driven by her chauffeur, Joe Thorpe, resplendent in dark green livery. Although a chauffeur/gardener Joe was every inch a gentleman.

On the left of the bridge, which was a favourite gathering place for the young of the village, stood a mill, owned by Mr. Topham. The awesome mill race could be seen and heard through a window set at ground level. The parapet of the bridge was capped with sandstone and every Sunday my father used to sharpen the carving knife on it. The worn stone remains to this day.

Next to the mill was a row of four cottages. I was born in the one nearest the mill and spent the rest of my childhood in the one at the other end of the row, which was slightly superior to the others as it had a garden at the side and a large wooden shed across the yard. Opposite was another large house, The Moat House, built of locally-made stock bricks in the early nineteenth century and owned by Mrs. Craig, a striking lady of Viennese extraction. Her garden continued along the line of the road till it joined the orchard belonging to the village shop. Next to our house, separated by a plot of land on which our next-door neighbour, Mr. Catlin, kept chickens, was a cobbler's shop owned by Jim Copps, who lived with his wife Annie and brother Noah next door but one to us. There was a long bench inside the window full of pairs of shoes of all descriptions waiting to be mended and Jim could be seen seated on an old wooden chair, wearing steel-rimmed glasses, flat cap on his head, and wearing a white carpenter's apron, a last gripped firmly between his knees, and a number of nails held in his mouth, taking them out one at a time and hammering them into the leather, the smell of which would fill the shop with a pleasant aroma. It was fascinating to watch him hammering home the nails with a large file, skilfully trimming the leather to shape with a sharp knife, smoothing off the edges and applying heel ball, before setting the shoe aside to dry off. There were then some more cottages, followed by the village shop, a few more cottages, and the old post office, with the "White Horse" Trust House opposite.

The village shop was owned by Mr. and Mrs. Rayment who had three sons, Reg, Eric, and Ralph. Reg and Eric both worked at the shop which was also a bakery. Eric, a young giant, delivered bread in a large square wicker basket carried over his arm, with a white cloth covering the bread. Reg did most of the baking and although smaller than Eric, had powerful shoulders and arms through continually pounding dough. Ralph was still at school and was therefore one of us.

Epcombs

The Mill, as it is today, and the house where I was born

The shop sold most things you would expect to find in a village shop, as well as yeast, and vinegar by the jug. A few jars of sweets, mostly boiled sweets and toffees, and Victory V lozenges, stood on a shelf in the window, and behind a glass-fronted cabinet were twelve tins of biscuits in two rows of six, their lids removed, displaying ginger nuts, jammy faces, Oval Osbornes, Sweet Marie, Nice, and other favourites. A lovely young lady named Dolly served in the shop and referred to us all, whatever our ages, as "Sir" or "Madam".

Outside the shop, jutting out from above the window and forming two sides of a triangle, was a large green sign with gold lettering proclaiming "Daren, the best brown bread", while fixed to the wall was a metal sign depicting an ocean liner leaving a white wake on a deep blue sea, with the legend "Out of the blue comes the whitest wash", advertising Reckitts Blue, which was the standard whitening agent when clothes were laundered in a copper boiler heated by a small fire.

Another sign read "Brooke Bond Tea". The tea was delivered to the shop in a Trojan van which had solid tyres and whose motor made a peculiar and distinctive burbling noise. Eric acquired an old second-hand Trojan van and learned to drive it round the orchard and we had great fun sitting in the back and being tossed about as it bounced over the rough grass.

Across the road in the orchard were geese, which hissed at us with outstretched necks as we passed, turkeys which raised their feathers and trotted menacingly towards us, and dozens of chickens. Ralph usually fed these and we would sometimes accompany him as he scattered corn, replenished the water bottles in the coops, and collected the eggs.

At this point the road climbs out of the valley and divides, St. Mary's Lane going off to the left to the church and railway station. The main road continues past a large house, "Amores", which was originally two separate timber-framed houses of the fifteenth century and converted into a single house in the sixteenth century, set in the angle between the two roads, to bend sharply right at "The Prince of Wales" public house on the right, while another lane to the left joins St. Mary's Lane by the church. Opposite "The Prince of

The house where I spent my childhood, with new extension

The village street from the "White Horse", with Rayment's shop on right

Wales'' by the junction with the lane stood Mrs. Hummerstone's sweet shop which was an Aladdin's Cave for small boys. Sherbert dabs, sugar mice, liquorice sticks, gobstoppers, toffee apples, prize packets, all on display in open boxes around the shop. Today such a shop would be closed as a health hazard but to my knowledge nobody's health ever suffered from eating sweets bought there. Some confectionery could be purchased from the village shop, previously mentioned, and the post office but to a small boy nothing could compare with Mrs. Hummerstone's.

A few yards along the lane leading to the church a huge walnut tree overhung the road from the garden of Garth House, a mid-eighteenth-century house whose cellars date from before 1630. When the walnuts were dropping we stood under the tree on Sundays before morning service, picking up the nuts as they fell, and when the church bell began to toll the last few minutes we would dash to church, change into our cassocks and surplices, and walk serenely, if breathlessly, into the choir stalls.

Continuing our journey through the village, there were a few more cottages to the left with King and Riddle's builders yard at the end, its timber sheds abutting the entrance to the allotments. On the right-hand side more cottages stood on a high bank, and finally, almost at the very end, stood the White Cottages, so-called because they were built of white brick, with the village post office at one end. The post office was a large wooden shed in the garden of the first house and one could purchase the better-quality sweets here including chocolate bars such as Double-Six, Fry's Sandwich, and Selection Bar, the latter being six chocolates with different centres joined together in one bar. It also sold bottles of Tizer, a favourite for drinking with Sunday lunch, or dinner as it was called then.

A path ran round the back of the cottages, past pairs of brick-built back-to-back earth closets, and in summertime it was a rather noisome place, to be avoided if at all possible. Joby Hart, the village strong man, lived in one of the cottages, next door to my grand-parents, and, together with Mr. Whiskin, caretaker of both the Memorial Hall and the village school, he would take part in boxing bouts in the Corn

The "White Horse"

Junction with St. Mary's Lane, with "Amores" just visible between the trees

Exchange at Hertford. At local fetes he could always be found performing feats of strength.

A double row of allotments, backed by a stand of Scots pines, led to the Cowper Memorial Hall which, as village halls go, was far superior to most other village halls in the country. Built on the instructions of Countess Cowper as a memorial to her husband, the Seventh Earl Cowper, it was aproached by a gravel drive with trees and shrubs on either side and with two beautifully-kept bowling rinks opposite the hall itself. One entered the hall from a large covered verandah, through double oak doors into a large oak-panelled room with a sprung maple dance floor. There was a stage at one end with an expensive grand piano and at the other end the heads of three water buffalos were mounted on the wall, trophies from Lord Desborough's safaris in Africa, something which we thought was quite normal then. Behind the stage was another oak-panelled room which was the working men's club, above which was the billiards room, again oak-panelled and with leaded windows looking out across the fields to the river. Linking the club room to the hall was a bar and behind this, and integral with the rest of the building, was the caretaker's accommodation.

A small bungalow adjoined the garden of the Memorial Hall and this was the home of my close childhood friend, Peter Hillyard. Peter and I spent many happy hours and days together, playing cricket, cycle riding, playing games down by the river and in the fields and woods. Peter was to become an engineer in adult life and even in those early days he displayed an aptitude for engineering. He was forever stripping down his bicycle to the ballbearings, cleaning and oiling every part, and making sure that everything was in good working order.

At the extreme edge of the village, set well back from the road, was Home Farm, always known to us as Campkin's Farm, after the brothers Stan and Ernie Campkin who lived there, and later on as Quenby's Farm when George Quenby and his family moved in..

To return to the bottom of the hill where the lane went off to the left, there was The Little Manor, a cross-wing late

The White Cottages showing the house where Granny lived

The Cowper Memorial Hall as it is today

sixteenth-early seventeenth century brick house with rendered front, two more cottages, then the tailor's shop, where Mr. Spratt could be seen sitting cross-legged in the window sewing suits. His suits were very expensive and were for the gentry of the area. Another row of cottages and then, just past a long driveway leading to The Old Rectory, the home of the Addis family, stood the church of St. Mary, large for a village, standing back from the lane among imposing yew trees. Next to the church was the sports field, always known as the cricket field, and one more field, belonging to the Sunday school teacher, separated this from the little railway station, through which passed the branch line from Hertford to Hatfield. The rectory, almost opposite the cricket pavilion, completes the layout of the village.

Many of the houses in the village belonged to the Panshanger Estate, the rent for which had to be paid monthly. For the sake of convenience rent could be paid at the village school and I was one of a small group of children who collected the rent from a number of houses and took it to school, along with the rent books, and paid it to the headmaster. In December the rent had to be paid as usual, but after the rent book had been signed the money was handed back as a Christmas box to the tenants. I took all the money back to the respective owners most of whom insisted on giving me a mince pie or a piece of cake and perhaps a glass of sherry or home-made wine. I returned home at the end of my round with rosy cheeks and feeling at peace with the world.

Milk was delivered by Mr. Woods in a small horse-drawn cart which was beautifully painted and spotlessly clean and carried churns of milk on the inside of which dangled two stainless steel measures with long handles, one for half a pint and the other for a pint. Mr. Woods, always smartly dressed and wearing a fore-and-aft leather hat, would ring a bell and call out "Milko" and people went out with their jugs to have the milk ladled into them. It was rich, creamy milk, and we never came to any harm through drinking it, although a number of children could be found at that time with scars on their necks where tubercular glands caused by drinking infected milk had been removed.

Throughout the year there were parties to celebrate friends' birthdays, when we dressed up in our party clothes, and turned up with hair neatly combed, clutching a small present. There were always jellies and fancy cakes, and plates full of finely cut sandwiches, and organised party games which we all enjoyed.

Once a year, near Christmas, the British Legion gave a large party for all the children of the village and the surrounding Greens in the Memorial Hall. The hall would be decorated with paper chains and a huge Christmas tree hung with coloured lights stood in one corner. We played party games, followed by a huge tea, and then later were entertained by a conjurer. Before we returned home everyone was given a nicely wrapped gift from under the Christmas tree, carefully selected for age and sex.

One year Dad presented the Christmas tree to the British Legion. Some years earlier he had planted our small Christmas tree in his allotment and it had taken root successfully. It had grown to about twelve feet high and had outgrown its space. It felt good to go to the party knowing that it was our tree which stood in the corner of the hall, resplendent in its array of tinsel and coloured lights.

Hertingfordbury, originally a late Saxon settlement, was designated a Conservation Area in 1968. Although basically the same village there have been many alterations. The shoe repairers and the village shop has gone, as has the post office and Mrs. Hummerstone's sweet shop. The "White Horse" is now a fairly large motel and the railway line went with the Beeching cuts in the 1960s. The station house has been rebuilt and bears no resemblance to the original, and the Memorial Hall, although used by organisations in the village, such as the Women's Institute, no longer functions as a Working Men's Club. Happily King and Riddle's yard, now owned by one of the original village boys, Harry Shepherd, who retails all kinds of vehicle electrical equipment, still retains its timber buildings and rustic village appearance.

Sadly, too, the bypass mentioned at the beginning of this chapter has replaced the old brick hump-backed with its overhanging alder tree. The river is now choked with weeds and the places where we used to paddle and swim are now unrecognisable. However, the fields remain and although new trees cover the spot where the old rubbish dump was the general aspect is still the same and without too much of a stretch to the imagination one is easily transported back in time to those wonderful childhood days.

2
My Home

MY HOME LIFE was a very happy one. My father and mother were both kind and loving parents, and I had a brother, John, who was nearly five years younger than I. Although poor we were never without good food and were always decently dressed, although I'm sure my parents sometimes made sacrifices and went without things in order to make ends meet. I can remember seeing my mother sitting at the table with a pencil and a piece of paper, money spread out before her, and crying.

As children we didn't have many toys but neither did we need or want them. With a simple tennis ball one could play five stones, catches, cricket, French cricket, hockey, football, and touch ball, a game where you had to throw the ball at someone and if you hit them they in turn had to try to hit someone else. A stick became a sword or a gun and our imaginations did the rest. Boredom was unknown.

My father, who worked for the County Council, was a very hard-working man. Luxury for him was to go to bed after Sunday lunch and rest till about five o'clock when mother would wake him up with a cup of tea. In addition to working outside in all weathers he had two allotments at the far end of the village and we always had fresh vegetables in season. Potatoes were stored in a boarded-off corner of the shed and ropes of onions hung along one side, under which stood the large wooden-rollered mangle and dad's bike. In another corner the coal was stacked, and in yet another corner, in a separate "room", was the privy.

Dad's allotments were a joy to behold with their immaculate weed-free rows of healthy vegetables: potatoes, onions, carrots, beetroot, shallots for pickling, runner beans, dwarf beans, peas, spinach, brussels sprouts and cabbages in succession, parsnips, and some of the crispest, sweetest celery you've ever tasted.

Beef and mutton were cheap in those days, pork and chicken only being bought for special occasions. We did, however, supplement our diet with the occasional pheasant, which we were told was chicken. Next to the allotment was an orchard in which pheasants roosted and they ravaged the young cabbage shoots. Dad's philosophy was that if Lord Desborough's pheasants were feeding on his greens he was entitled to some of Lord Desborough's pheasants. He would go to the allotment after dark, see the pheasants silhouetted against the night sky and bring them down with a stone from his catapult.

This catapult was something special. It was beautifully formed from a piece of mahogany. As a schoolboy he had made it in the woodwork shop when he was supposed to have been making a bookcase, and was a crack shot with it. The good thing about any pheasant or rabbit brought down in this manner was that there were no nasty little bits of lead shot to pick out and death was swift and clean.

As previously mentioned our house was slightly superior to the others in the row as we were end of terrace which made us in effect semi-detached, and whereas the other houses were two up and two down we had a large scullery which gave us much more space. The scullery had a quarry-tiled floor and a stone kitchen sink with a pump which drew water from a well in the yard. There was a copper built into one corner and a large floor-to-ceiling cupboard in the opposite corner. There was also a gas cooker, a Welsh dresser, and a large kitchen table. All of this meant that our living room was much more comfortable and warm, having no outside door to it.

Christmas was a very special time at home. On Christmas Eve the fire was lit in the front room and the Christmas tree was placed in a large china pot in the corner and decorated. Paper chains were hung around the room, sprigs of holly were tucked behind pictures, and there was always a bunch of mistletoe over the door between the front room and the living room.

My brother and I would go to bed early, too excited to sleep yet afraid to stay awake in case Father Christmas didn't come. Early on Christmas morning we would probe tentatively with our toes to feel the parcels at the foot of the bed, all wrapped in brown paper and tied with string, and just as exciting as today's multi-coloured ones.

Christmas lunch was also very special, with a nice roast cockerel, roast potatoes and parsnips, brussels sprouts, and stuffing, followed by Christmas pudding and custard. After lunch we all retired to the front room to listen to the king's speech on the radio. Tea consisted of plates of thin bread and butter, both white and brown, cheese, and celery, the celery being in a large glass celery jar in the centre of the table. This was followed by Christmas cake and mince pies. Sometimes one or two of my parents' friends came to tea and a companionable evening would be spent in the front room with a glass or two of port, swapping yarns and requesting the occasional song from Jim, a Yorkshireman with a fine tenor voice.

My mother's cakes were legendary. There was always home-made cake in the house - cherry, mixed fruit, caraway seed, Madeira, and jam sponges - and portions were always generous. She was also an excellent pastry cook.

There were several uncles and aunts on my mother's side living in the area but I didn't see much of them. My favourite visitors were my Granny and Granddad, my mother's parents, and my Aunt Edie, who was my father's only sister. Granny and Granddad usually called in on Saturday evenings after going shopping at Hertford. As they had to walk the two miles carrying their shopping our house was a welcome stopping point for a cup of tea and a chat before they continued on their way to the other end of the village. Aunt Edie usually cycled over to see us at all sorts of times and always brought whipped cream walnuts and a peach for my brother and me. She had a Brownie box camera and must have taken hundreds of snaps of us as children.

Our next-door neighbours were Mr. and Mrs. Catlin. Mr. Catlin, a tall man with a slight stoop, was a baker at Rayment's shop and occasionally brought me a small loaf, made from a small piece of dough left over from the main baking, which he called a "dodger". I am surprised now that he was so kind to me because, as a small boy, I would stand watching him at work in his back yard, making something or other, and just at the moment he reached out to pick up a tool I would snatch it up and run away with it. He'd chase me and just before he caught me I would throw it over into the chicken run.

Mrs. Catlin was a lovely lady with white hair and steel-rimmed glasses, who always wore a spotless white apron. We often went next door for afternoon tea and there was always a choice of Sweet Marie or Oval Osborne biscuits.

I remember us getting our first radio. I'm not quite sure of the year but it was after the wedding of the Duke of Kent and Princess Marina because we went next door to Mrs. Catlin's to hear that. The radio was a large wooden affair with a high tension battery, a smaller grid bias battery, and an acid accumulator. These accumulators had to be carried to Hertford about once a fortnight to be recharged and woe betide you if it touched your clothes, which would drop into holes a short time later.

The radio brought a new dimension to our lives. We could listen to the wonderful dance orchestras of the time: Henry Hall, Jack Payne, Roy Fox, and Carrol Gibbons and the Savoy Hotel Orpheans. There was Uncle Mac on Children's Hour and evening programmes such as "Monday Night at Seven" and "In Town Tonight". For a very long time I really believed that the BBC had stopped London's traffic in order to talk to people in the street.

There were accordian bands, harmonica bands, wonderful Hawaiian music, and cowboy songs which gave the impression that a cowboy's life was a very romantic one instead of the hard grind that it is in reality.

We also had our favourite comedy stars, such as Arthur Askey and Dickie Murdoch, Wheeler and Woolsey, and a host of others.

When I was about six years old a new member joined the family in the shape of a puppy. Trix, as he was called, was a cross between a Pomeranian and another type of terrier. He had a beautiful fox-red head with silky fur, a chocolate-coloured back, toning down to a creamy-fawn underside, and delightful little plus fours on his back legs. He became *my* dog, forming that close bond which occurs between children and animals. When my father went downstairs first thing in the morning to make the tea, as soon as he opened the door at the foot of the stairs Trix would come bounding up, jump on to my bed, and burrow to the bottom by my feet. No amount of pushing and prodding on my part would make him move.

He loved to ride through the village on Dad's wheelbarrow, standing with his front paws on the curved front, king of all he surveyed. When we were both a little older I taught him to ride on the carrier of my bicycle. He sat there like a seasoned pillion rider, leaning into the corners with his ears flattened to his head. I would take him to visit my Aunt Edie, who lived five miles away, in this manner, with just a lead from him to my hand in case he fell off, which he never did.

We often went for long circular walks but as he got older he would suddenly decide that he'd walked far enough, turn round and go home. Sometimes we were well over half way round but as far as he was concerned his was the quicker way.

A main sewerage drain was laid through the village when I was about eleven years old. This involved digging a massive trench down one side of the road and a pumping station was built next door to us on what was previously Mr. Catlin's chicken run. The work lasted for many weeks and the night watchman, a Mr. Watts, known to everyone as "Old Wattie", made the pumping station his base. Every evening, just before dusk, he went round the village lighting all the red lamps by the side of the trench. That task finished he returned to his tarpaulin shack and glowing brazier. My brother and I often went and sat with him for a while, breathing in the coke fumes and sucking the home-made cough drops which he gave us, whilst listening to some of his yarns. We hung on to his every word and his tales of "life" were far more interesting than the academic subjects we were forced to study at school.

The building of the pumping station brought several benefits for us. Our shed had to be moved so much of it was renewed, and eventually a w.c. was installed in place of the old earth closet, and a tap put in the scullery to replace the pump.

One of my earliest memories is, at the age of about three, of sitting in my grandparents' garden on a small patch of grass, and watching the bees gathering nectar from a large red-flowering currant bush.

Another early memory is of being taken to visit my father's parents who lived at Westmill, a small village about five miles away. Dad took me on the carrier of his bicycle and the route was along an unmade-up lane. It was quite exciting hanging on as we skirted the potholes but one part of the ride always terrified me. Almost at the end of the journey the road crossed the river on which stood the mill from which the village took its name. The mill race roared out from beneath the mill and under the bridge with just some railings between road and water. I held on for dear life until we were safely across.

My father's parents were rather sterner than my other grandparents. Granny was an austere, straight-backed lady who had spent many years in gentlemens' service. On arrival she always offered me a glass of "Eiffel Tower" lemonade which she served in a barrel-shaped tumbler and I would sit there sipping it and watching the pendulum of the grandmother clock swinging backwards and forwards, ticking away the seconds. By a trick of the light it appeared to twist at the end of its swing and this never ceased to fascinate me.

Grandfather was a rather taciturn man and I regarded him with some awe, at least until I was old enough to get to know him better.

Two or three hundred yards down the road from where my grandparents lived was a small farmhouse called Paynes Hall where my Uncle Bert and Aunt Emma lived and we often visited them at the same time. Aunt Emma was my mother's oldest sister and she was a jolly lady. She had five children, one boy and four girls, the oldest girl being almost the same age as my mother, but the two youngest, Peggy and Joyce, were nearer my age and being tomboys were always good fun to visit.

Uncle Bert kept goats and it was here that I was introduced to goat's milk which I found rather rich but not unpleasant. When I was a few years older and had my own bicycle, I used to make these visits on my own on a fairly regular basis.

3
The School

THE SCHOOL was not in the village but a mile away at Birch Green, and served all the other small hamlets in the area, Staines Green, Letty Green, Cole Green, East End Green, Labby Green, and Roxford. The building was in the style of the times, made of red brick, with large diamond-leaded windows set high in the wall, making it impossible to see out. The school catered for the complete age range, from five to leaving time at fourteen. The "mixed and infants" classes were ably taught by Miss Bolton, a lady who had also taught my mother in her schooldays, and catered for children up to the age of eight.

Under the capable tutelage of Miss Bolton we were taught to read and write, to tell the time, and to learn our "times tables", a built-in ready reckoner which has proved invaluable for the rest of our lives. In the final year in her class we learnt to make papier-mâche bowls and rush mats, decorate boxes with eggshell mosaic, and make corded seats for stools, using seagrass. I have a lovely memory of Miss Bolton measuring out the yards of seagrass using the tip of her nose to the end of her arm as a yard measure.

The middle classes, Standards 2, 3, and 4, taught by Mrs. Rayment, the headmaster's wife, were for children aged eight to eleven. These classes concentrated on improving our reading and writing skills and botany and nature study were brought into the curriculum. Good spelling was considered a "must" and each spelling mistake had to be written out six times and handed in for checking.

The top classes, Standards 5 to 7, taught by Mr. Rayment, took one through to school leaving. Here, in addition to reading, writing, and arithmetic we were taught drawing, technical drawing, and map making which included making large-scale maps of various parts of the village showing field boundaries and crops. For these maps we used waxed linen, drawing the maps with mapping pens on the front of the sheet and brushing various coloured inks, representing grass, corn, trees, etc., on the back. There was one particular occasion when we were preparing a map showing the acidity or alkalinity of various fields. This involved a certain amount of field study, getting samples of soil and taking them back to school for analysis. Groups of three or four were allocated an area for sampling. My particular group thought it would be fun to hurry back to school with our sample and add some lime from the garden store. Ours was the only alkaline sample from an otherwise very acidic field. It was put down on the records as a freak pocket.

There were two playgrounds, strictly segregated, the lower and middle classes using one and the three senior classes using the other. This was probably done for reasons of safety as the senior children were always playing rough games such as hockey, played with a wooden puck and any sort of stick one could lay one's hands on. Favourite sticks were hidden in all sorts of places - under the water butt, under the woodwork shop, in gutters, etc. - and these were hastily but covertly sought out each time a game was imminent.

In one corner of the infants' playground was an L-shaped building known as the mess rooms. At one time this was where the children ate their sandwiches but during my time at school they were used for storing games equipment. A narrow path ran round the back of the mess rooms and this was a place for clandestine meetings. There was a certain girl at the school who shall forever remain anonymous, but if any boy upset his fellows for some reason or other he had to go behind the mess rooms and kiss this girl as a punishment. Funnily enough, I can't ever remember the girl objecting.

Hanging on the wall in one of the rooms was a picture of two chimpanzees wearing striped bathing costumes and standing on a diving board. The large chimpanzee had his foot planted firmly on the back of his small companion and the caption read "Sink or swim". These words have remained with me as a salutary reminder of what life is really like.

The school at Birch Green

Dad's catapult

Mr. Rayment had been an army captain in World War I and the school tended to be run on military lines. Boys were required to salute when they passed him and on Empire Day we were all assembled in the playground and then marched round the school to salute the flag, flying from a flagpole above the school. This ceremony over we were dismissed to have the rest of the day off. It was a bit of a bind for those living in outlying villages to have to walk to school only to have the walk home again about half an hour later. For the Bury boys, and girls, as we were known, Ascension Day was the worst. We first had to walk the mile and a bit to school for assembly, march back down to the church for the service, march once more to the school to be dismissed, and then walk back to the village again, as being a church school the rest of the day was a holiday.

Nevertheless, school days were on the whole very enjoyable, and the head, although strict, was fair, and often joined in the fun in the playground. In the winter we were allowed to pour water on the playground before we went home in the afternoon, which froze overnight, and the next morning we had slides in which he joined, but woe betide any boy who went on the slide wearing studded boots, which "cut candles", or rubber soled shoes or wellingtons which dulled the surface. After the fun we had to sprinkle ashes where the slide passed the entrance to the school gardens and the woodwork and cookery huts.

The gardens were the headmaster's pride and joy. Surrounded by a high privet hedge, the first section contained flower beds and lawns, while the second part was for vegetables and fruit trees. One of the tasks every winter was to draw a scale plan of the garden and draw in lines in different colours representing which vegetables were to be grown and where. Once springtime came and digging and raking began in earnest, these plans were religiously adhered to. Another winter job was to spray the fruit trees with a tar oil winter wash. This was done by means of large brass pressure sprays with flexible hoses and adjustable nozzles. The sprays had to be pumped up to a certain pressure, shown by a pressure gauge mounted on the top of the tank. There was a red line marked on the scale which was the danger point for pressure, and it was always a point of honour to exceed this mark as far as we dared. Once pressure was achieved the appliance was placed on one boy's back and held there with shoulder straps whilst his partner held the hose and sprayed the trees. As may be imagined, when several boys were spraying trees in the same area there was inevitably some horseplay, and many a boy went home with hair and clothes reeking of tar oil.

We were taught pruning, grafting, and budding, and records were kept of the amount of growth each tree made during the year, the number of blossom trusses per tree, and the amount of fruit obtained. Charts were made and some of these, together with specimens of grafting, were entered in the Royal Show, and occasionally gained commendations.

Great emphasis was placed on country matters and there were country walks, and occasionally school outings to places such as Royston Heath, where we sought out and catalogued all the different wild flowers and grasses which could be found.

There were other outings too, partly educational and partly recreational. One such outing was to Welwyn Garden City to see the film "David Copperfield". The highlight of the evening for the boys, however, was not the film but the sight of that great steam engine, the "Night Scotsman", roaring through the night on its way to Scotland, leaving a trail of red sparks in its wake.

Another memorable outing was to London with a visit first of all to the Imperial War Museum, then to Buckingham Palace to see the changing of the guard, followed by a boat trip from Tower Pier to the docks, which were then a hive of activity with ships from all over the world unloading and taking on cargo.

One of the great days in the school calendar was the annual ploughing match and hedging and ditching competition which took place on one of the local farms. This was for the senior classes only and we were left to do very much as we liked so long as we took plenty of notes and asked lots of questions as the crunch came the following day when a comprehensive essay had to be written about the day's events. The soil of the area was very heavy, having a band of London Clay running through it which was fine for the heavy iron ploughs but very difficult for one poor man from Sussex who turned up year after year with a wooden plough which was eminently suitable for his local sandy soil but presented him with all kinds of problems elsewhere. He was forever having to stop and clean the plough with a stick but he always won a prize for being in a special class, so I suppose it was worth his while to attend.

Apart from gardening the boys were taught woodwork while the girls were taught domestic science, including sewing, needlework, and cookery. Once a year the school held a sale of work and for weeks beforehand the girls were busy making dolls and golliwogs, children's clothing, and evening bags, and making clothes for and dressing little celluloid dolls. Meanwhile the boys would be busy in the woodwork shop making beds for the dolls, for which the girls made bedclothes, little sheets and blankets and patchwork quilts. Everything was sold and the proceeds went to the county hospital.

Sport was catered for, the boys playing cricket and football, and the girls rounders and netball, and occasionally there were field sports such as running and jumping, but it was all carried on in a carefree manner, more for fun than competition. Football tended to be a bit of an ordeal as in those days footballs were made of leather and the field in which we played was unmown, so that on wet days the ball soon became as heavy as lead. Football boots were made of leather with leather studs and covered in a viscous coat of dubbin, while shinguards were thick magazines stuffed down our socks and held in place by black elastic garters.

This was the only cloud on the horizon during my school days. The memory of running, or rather stumbling, up and down the wing in long wet grass in the middle of winter remains to this day and in consequence I have never been a follower of football.

The school was part of the Panshanger Estate, owned by Lord and Lady Desborough, and once a year in the early autumn the children were invited to tea at the big house, together with the children from Tewin school, which was also part of the estate. On arrival we assembled on the lawns in front of the house. The great man then appeared and scattered liquorice comfits for us to scramble for, a memory which now makes me cringe. We then went into the house for a sit-down tea and afterwards were treated to some sort of entertainment, usually a conjurer or a Punch and Judy show. We were handed a bag of sticky sweets and an orange as we left and made our way home, the older children walking home through the woods looking for glowworms and the younger children being taken home in the Rolls Royce.

Just before the school broke up for the Christmas holidays there was the annual school concert and prizegiving. This took place in the Cowper Memorial Hall. The infants always presented The Rainbow Concert Party, where all the children were dressed in multi-coloured costumes made from tissue paper and performed their songs and recitations. The contributions of the middle classes were usually choral works and perhaps a short comedy sketch, while the seniors sometimes performed an excerpt from one of Shakespeare's plays, such as the Woodcutter's Play from "A Midsummer Night's Dream", and played tunes on handbells.

Immediately following the concert was the prizegiving ceremony when prizes were given for 1st and 2nd in each class throughout the school, with special prizes for subjects such as Scripture. The books for first in class were presented by The Lady Desborough, who was lady-in-waiting to Queen Mary, and the rest by the school managers. There was also a cup presented for the most popular boy or girl in the school. The proud parents applauded all the acts and prizewinners and it was a very popular annual event.

St. Mary's Church, Hertingfordbury

Harry Shepherd's workshop

4
The Church

THE CHURCH OF ST. MARY, built of flint with stone dressing, and with a thirty-foot copper-clad steeple, green with verdigris, standing atop a sixty-foot tower, formed an integral part of village life. A church had stood on the site since the thirteenth century and several parts of the old church were incorporated into the new. It was extensively restored in 1890 by the Seventh Earl and Countess Cowper of Panshanger, who added the memorial chapel to the Cowper family. St. Mary's is a large church for a small village which reflects the number of landed gentry who lived in the area and contributed to its building and furnishing. The altar rails were carved from alabaster and the floor was of Italian marble tiles. The rich and beautiful velvet altar cloths, also from Italy, were presented to the church by one of the wealthy ladies of the village. All the woodwork, including the pews and the pulpit, were carved in the German town of Oberammagau, home of the passion play which is re-enacted there every ten years. The carpenter was one Josef Mayer, and one year we were given a talk on the passion play, illustrated by magic lantern slides, in which Josef Mayer played the part of Christ.

The church possessed a magnificent communion set made of solid gold. This was kept in a bank vault for most of the year but was brought out for Easter communion. On one never-to-be-forgotten day the members of the choir were allowed to hold the chalice. We were astounded by the sheer weight of it and it was probably the most expensive thing I will ever hold in my hand.

There were originally five bells in the belfry but after World War II the bells, which had been taken down during the hostilities, were re-hung and a sixth added by Mr. and Mrs.

Gregory of "Amores" in memory of their son who was killed while serving in the Royal Air Force.

I joined the choir at the age of seven not only for the joy of singing but also because we were paid. We received one penny for morning service, one penny for evening service, and a halfpenny for choir practice. Weddings were looked forward to eagerly as we were paid one shilling for singing at a wedding and if it was a village wedding there was the possibility of being invited to the reception for a free feast but we were expected to attend funerals for nothing as a mark of respect. There were no street lights in the village then but just inside the church gate was a gas lamp which was lit when the church was in use. This cast a yellow circle of light but served no more useful purpose than as a point to aim for. Walking through a dark churchyard, the path overhung by yew trees, could have been a daunting experience for a seven-year-old, but in those days there was nothing living to be afraid of, and certainly nothing dead could hurt you and so the churchyard was no more of a frightening place than one's own back yard.

The organist and choirmaster was a Mr. Kenerall, known to all as Jimmy, and although he was extremely deaf so far as conversation was concerned, he had a wonderful ear for music. The choir stalls were arranged two either side of the aisle, just in front of the altar. The women and girls sat in the back row on one side and took their seats before the service started. The boys and men processed into church in pairs and the boys sat in the two front pews while the men sat in the back row next to the organ. Boys being what they are we frequently whispered to each other during the sermon, to be stopped in our tracks by a heavy bible being dropped on our heads by one of the men sitting behind us. At weddings we sat and stared at the pair being married and their eyes travelled anywhere except in our direction.

At one time a new tenor joined the choir and he insisted on stressing certain notes in accordance with the way they were sung on BBC radio, contrary to the way we had traditionally been used to. This led to a big row in the vestry one evening which culminated in the whole choir being dismissed. The following Sunday morning the choir sat in the congregation in the front pew which led to an immediate inquiry as to the reason and we were reinstated the following week. We should, of course, have backed the choir master but young shoulders do not have wise heads on them.

After choir practice the boys would slip out quickly and after wetting their hands in the rainwater butt outside the vestry, hide in the yew trees which lined the path and reach out and touch the girls on their faces as they walked by. Although they knew what to expect they always ran screaming down the path. One evening during choir practice some of the village lads who were not in the choir came into the church and kept flashing torches up on the ceiling. This did not go unnoticed by Jimmy who walked down the darkened church to investigate. We could hear the kneeling rests being overturned as the boys scampered about to avoid detection, but poor old Jimmy could hear none of this and the boys evaded discovery.

Just over the fence at the back of the church were the large grounds of "The Fobury", the home of the Addis family, and about a third of the distance between the church and the house stood a French walnut tree. The nuts from this tree were very large and we would climb over the fence and run down to pick up as many as we could before we were spotted from the house. The Addises owned a Red Setter dog which seemed huge to us at that age, and directly we were spotted picking up walnuts the dog was set loose and the race was on to reach the fence and climb over before the dog reached us. I can only remember one boy being bitten. The following morning at school, however, the incident having been reported, we were all lined up for a hand inspection for the tell-tale yellow stains. The most wonderful excuses were invented for the cause of these stains and although we received a warning nothing could ever be proved conclusively.

Climbing to the top of the church tower was quite an adventure. Firstly one had to ascend the long stone spiral staircase to the ringing chamber. A further flight led up to the bell chamber, from where one had to climb a short ladder, walk along a narrow platform between the bells, then climb a steep ladder which terminated at a trapdoor in the side of the steeple. A stomach-churning step off the ladder and through the trapdoor and one was standing on the narrow stonework between the steeple and the battlements of the tower. The view from here was wonderful but it seemed a lot further from the top of the tower to the bottom than it did in the opposite direction.

One of the necessary jobs in the church was that of organ blower. The bellows were pumped by means of a long wooden handle protruding through the wall at the side of the organ and next to the handle was a lead weight on the end of a piece of string which was attached to the top of the bellows. As the bellows filled the lead weight descended. The idea was to pump the handle until the lead weight reached a line drawn on the wall which indicted that the bellows were fully inflated and then rest for a moment as the weight slowly rose, to recommence pumping before the weight passed another line higher up the wall, indicating that the bellows were nearly empty. Occasionally, if the organ blower was away for some reason or other, a senior boy from the choir was asked to pump. It then became *de rigueur* to allow the weight to ascend past the top line just far enough for the organ note to drop slightly and to receive a hard look from the organist.

"Jimmy" played the organ with feeling, using the stops with good effect to produce delightful variations of tone and pumping for him was relatively easy. Occasionally, however, Mr. Wheatley, the organist from the church at Letty Green, played at St. Mary's and he believed in pulling out all the stops, causing the lead weight to ascend rapidly. The organ blower certainly earned his money on these occasions.

As Christmas approached there was an air of suppressed excitement among the members of the choir. We practised all the well-known carols with great emphasis being placed on getting the pauses and the volume right. About two weeks before Christmas we went carol singing to raise money. Half of the proceeds went to charity and the other half for a choir party. We sang only at the big houses as they gave us a minimum of five shillings and often a ten-shilling or pound note. We probably sang at ten houses in the course of the evening and were often invited to sing inside and afterwards given glasses of sherry and slices of cake. After several such visits we felt warm and relaxed and by the time we reached the last house I'm certain we could have sung all night.

We sang in the village on one evening and at the Greens on perhaps two other occasions, as the Greens were rather strung out. The choir was always welcome wherever it went as it always gave value for money, singing at least three carols in full.

The church also owned a set of handbells with charts written out for the better-known hymns and carols to be played in harmony. Sometimes the men and the older boys and girls went out bellringing and it was wonderful to hear the bells ringing out on the frosty air of a clear moonlit night.

A regular feature of the church calendar was the annual Toy Service, held on the Sunday before Christmas, when we took toys to church, some new, some second-hand - favourite teddy bears, dolls, jigsaw puzzles, cigarette card albums, etc. - all to be given to the poor children of a parish in London. The service was always conducted by the Reverend Roland Smith and his theme was the same every year - empty vessels make the most sound. He illustrated his point with a popgun which made a lot of noise but was otherwise absolutely useless, a point over which we used to ponder as we grew older.

When Christmas Day arrived the church was decorated with flowers and sprays of holly and conifer branches. Two huge Christmas trees, festooned with coloured lights, stood one each side of the altar. Far more people attended church then than do today and the church would be fairly full for the morning service, after which the congregation, all warmly dressed in their Sunday best, stood for a few minutes in the churchyard wishing each other a Merry Christmas, before going home for Christmas dinner, which was the highlight of the year.

At the time I joined the choir in 1933 the rector was the Reverend Kingston, a kindly man who after choir practice in the summer used to invite the older boys and girls back to the rectory to play tennis on his private tennis court. He died several years later and was superseded by the Reverend Bond, a young man with modern ideas. He was the first parson we had seen wearing an open-necked shirt.

One of his introductions to the church was "the red hymn book" which contained about a dozen modern hymns with lively tunes, quite a change from the traditional ones we had been brought up with.

He chose me to sing the part of the page boy in "Good King Wenceslas". I found this a nerve-wracking experience at first, walking out into the aisle and singing before the congregation, but Mr. Bond, who took the part of the king, had a firm but gentle hand on my shoulder and gave me the occasional reassuring squeeze.

When war broke out he joined the army as a padre and after the war was over he decided to give up the ministry and became a market gardener in New Zealand.

5
The Fliers

ONE OF MY EARLIEST MEMORIES is of standing in my grandmother's garden and looking up to see an airship flying overhead. This turned out to be the R100, which was made at the de Havilland factory at Hatfield, only six miles away. The well-known novelist Nevil Shute, whose full name was Nevil Shute Norway and who was skilled in aeronautics, was engaged on this project. Living so near to such a well-known airport, we were naturally interested in all matters pertaining to aircraft. It was the time of the great aerial adventures. Jim Mollison, Amy Johnson, Amelia Earhart, and Campbell Black, who was married to the impressionist Florence Desmond, were all breaking records by flying to distant parts of the globe in small aircraft, and we listened breathlessly to the wireless or eagerly scanned the daily papers for news of their latest arrival at some remote outpost of the empire.

Now and again, not on a regular basis, a flying display took place in one of the fields just outside the village. The field was owned by Stan and Bill Campkin, two local characters, and was always known as Campkin's Field. The 'planes, mainly Avro biplanes, would fly in, the pilots clad in leather jackets and leather flying helmets, usually with silk scarves wrapped around their necks. One year the great Campbell Black himself attended, his black and silver monoplane being the centre of attraction. He was unfortunately killed some time later when his 'plane drove into the path of an airliner at Croydon.

There were usually two men at the field gate taking the money and handing out entry tickets. We boys didn't pay to go in, of course. We would circumnavigate the field, looking for a weak spot in the hedge, then quickly wriggle through and mingle with the crowd. We were never caught.

The mechanics would swing the propellers, the pilots rev up the engines, and the 'planes taxi bumpily over the rough grass of the field and take off. Then followed amazing displays of aerobatics, loop-the-loops, spiralling spins, rolls and dives, followed by a flypast upside down about a dozen feet from the ground right in front of the crowd. There were pleasure trips, usually a flight to the church and back, and there was one occasion when the oldest inhabitant of the village, a Mr. Cutts, aged 80, was taken for a free trip. There was a picture of him in the local weekly paper, *The Hertfordshire Mercury,* showing him sitting in the front cockpit with his flat cap pressed firmly down on his head. Some time during the course of the show balloons were released and the 'planes flew among them bursting them with their propellers. Sometimes a pilot, armed with a pistol, would fly at a target and break plates by shooting at them as he flew past.

The highlight of the day though, if weather conditions were considered to be right, was a wing walk and parachute jump, as in those days parachuting was a much more hazardous operation than it is today. We watched as the 'plane circled round until it reached a certain height, then a man would appear from the cockpit and walk along the wing, holding tightly to the struts and bracing wires. We all watched spellbound as he launched himself into space and held our breaths until we saw the large white parachute unfurl and he was swinging safely down to ground.

It was during this period that de Havilland's achieved a major breakthrough in aeroplane design with the manufacture of the de Havilland Comet. This was the first single winged aeroplane that did not employ struts either above or below the wing for stabilisation, and used what was known as the stressed wing design. It was quite revolutionary and very fast. It was advertised as going to appear at the flying display that year but in the event the landing speed was too fast for the small field and we had to be content with a fly past.

The morning after the display we cycled up to the field to inspect the 'planes at close quarters. The mechanics, with oily rags dangling from their trouser pockets, would be fussing around, tightening up nuts, checking sparking plugs, etc., while the pilots sat in the cockpits doing something to the controls. Eventually everything would be in order. The mechanic brought the propeller round to a position where the pilot called out "Contact", gave it a good swing and the engine would fire, blue smoke pouring out from the short exhaust pipes. After a short warming up period the mechanic pulled the chocks away from the wheels and climbed into the front cockpit, the 'plane bumped slowly across the field, the pilot gave it full throttle and after a relatively short run the 'plane was airborne and off they flew until another year.

Another easily recognisable de Havilland aeroplane was the Dragon Rapide. This reliable biplane, with its pointed wings and wheel spats, was used as a mail plane, and one could set one's watch by it as it flew over every evening. Aeroplanes were all beautifully coloured in those days, metallic reds, blues, and greens, as well as the basic silver, and I think the Rapide was a beautiful red and silver.

Once a year the King's Cup Air Race took place and we could observe the race from the cricket field. The 'planes flew on a circular course, and took off at intervals on a handicap basis, so that in theory, all things being equal, they should all finish at the same time. This was where good flying skills and navigation came in and we would watch each circuit and note the changing positions as the more experienced pilots gradually moved into the lead.

Although, sadly, no longer in existence, de Havilland's will always be remembered as one of the great pioneers in aircraft development.

In addition to our interest in real aircraft we had great fun in making and flying model aeroplanes. These were basically a straight piece of wood for the fuselage, with open-framed wings covered with oiled silk and driven by a thick rubber band hooked on to a piece of wire at the tail end and joined to the propeller at the other. These models had to be held very firmly whilst the elastic was being wound up and there was many a rapped finger caused by being careless during this operation.

We also played at being aeroplanes, using winter warmers for engines. For these you required cocoa tins and some old rags. Cocoa tins were made entirely of metal and as cocoa was one of the staple drinks these were readily obtainable. As for the rags, almost every house had a rag bag in which all discarded clothing was put after the buttons had been cut off and put in a button tin. As a small child I spent many wonderful hours sorting through the exotic-looking buttons in mother's button tin. The rags could be used for cleaning bicycles, garden tools, and all manner of things.

Sheets, too, after they had been turned sides to middle and were finally too thin to be used for bedding, were boiled and ironed and put away to be used in place of handkerchiefs when we had colds, after which they were burned, or for bandages, frequently required to cover skinned knees and elbows.

But I digress. To make the winter warmers one made a series of small holes in the tin lid and one larger hole in the bottom of the tin. The tin was then stuffed with old rags and set alight. Once the flame had taken hold it was blown out leaving the rags smouldering. The lid was then put on the tin and, with one in each hand, with the lid facing forward, we would run around the fields leaving trails of smoke behind us and at the same time warming our hands as the tins became progressively hotter.

6
The "White Horse"

THERE WEREN'T MANY BOYS in the village and we all tended to play together. We looked upon ourselves as a gang, the Bury Boys, and the boys from the Greens, although we played with them in the playground at school, at all other times they were a race apart, to be treated with suspicion. Two of the boys, John and George Lambert, lived at the Trust House, the "White Horse", and this was usually the base for most of our activities.

The "White Horse" was originally a sixteenth-century timber-framed Wealden type house with a brick front added in the eighteenth century and was a small inn with a large garden to one side and a spacious car park on the other. To the rear of the car park was a sizeable wooden building, once stables. At one end was the tea room and at the other a garage for the landlord's car, one of the few cars in the village. Above the tea room and garage was a loft, with sides open to the elements, and it was here that we gathered on wet days. There was a swing rigged up from the beams and when in use one's legs swung out into space. Had you let go of the ropes you would have been launched into eternity.

Sometimes we pooled our pocket money and bought two or three Woodbine cigarettes and took them to the loft, where they would be cut into small pieces and either smoked as they were or placed into little pipes we made from acorns and pieces of straw. We felt really big and manly as we puffed away at the weed. At times, if we could not afford to buy cigarettes, we picked up cigarette ends from the car park, trimmed off the burnt ends, and smoked these, and, even worse, sometimes tried to smoke dried onion leaves.

Behind the tea room was a large stand of cycle racks, and at weekends these would be full as those were the days of the Cycling Tourist Club and groups of cyclists, perhaps forty or fifty at a time, resplendent in plus fours and diamond patterned pullovers and socks, descended on the village. Many of these clubs came from London and the country was a refreshing change from the rows of houses and busy streets. On the Hertford side of the village was a large bluebell wood, part of the Panshanger Estate, and the cyclists would walk up to the woods and pick armsful of bluebells and cycle back to London with their carriers loaded with the wilting blue flowers.

We were always engaged on some kind of project and there was one particular boy, who shall not be named, who was invariably nominated to try out our latest venture. Once we spent several days working away at making a punt. We sawed the wood to shape and hammered in the nails and when the punt was finally made it was covered all over with pitch to make it waterproof. After allowing the pitch time to dry we carried it in triumph across the fields to the river. The structure was placed at the edge of the water, our "guinea pig" was installed in its centre, and it was duly launched. It glided majestically into the deeper water and slowly sank.

We spent days looking over rubbish dumps for old prams and pushchairs so that we could take off the wheels to make a trolley. Two pairs of wheels, one pair preferably larger than the other, were fixed to a plank of wood, the larger pair at the back and screwed firmly on, and the smaller pair at the front bolted through the centre of the axle so that they could swivel. Sometimes as a refinement a soapbox was nailed on the top to form a seat. A crude wooden brake completed the ensemble. Many happy hours were spent pushing each other around or freewheeling down one of the hills.

A lot of time was spent playing in the "White Horse" gardens where we had a more or less free run outside licensing hours. At the top of the garden was a large laburnam tree in which we built a tree hut. We had great fun making the hut and playing in it until one day too many tried to get in at once and we had to scamper quickly down the tree as the hut disintegrated.

At the edge of the garden was the trunk of a large walnut tree which had been felled. The branches had been removed but the trunk was too heavy and bulky to be taken away. It was at the time when Bing Crosby was making his name as a crooner and one day John Lambert spent nearly all the afternoon standing on the trunk pretending to be Bing and singing all his latest hits.

At one time the "White Horse" had a large refrigerator installed. This involved the digging of a cooling well outside in the yard and large circular wooden formers about six feet across and about three feet wide were used in its construction. Now these formers were wonderful toys. We could stand inside one of them and walk so that it rolled across the car park. Someone had the bright idea that if we took it across the fields to the top of the hill we could roll it down. This was done and our victim was placed inside the former with feet braced at the bottom and hands clasping the open boards at the top. We then set it rolling down the hill where it rapidly gathered speed until it hit a bump and turned over onto its side. This was probably just as well for the hill was about two hundred yards long and if the former had rolled the full length the outcome could well have been fatal.

The "White Horse" made its own ice cream and it was, and still is, the most delicious ice cream I've ever tasted. Cream was poured into a container set in a tub packed with ice and with a geared handle at the side. The whole contraption was stood on an old wooden chair and we took it in turns to turn the handle. As the cream began to thicken turning the handle became really hard work, but when the ice cream was eventually ready all the helpers were given a spoonful for their pains and the boy who did the most work was given the mixing paddle and a spoon and had a real feast.

Mr. and Mrs. Lambert, the proprietors of the "White Horse", were very kind to the village lads. At times when we were playing in the garden Mrs. Lambert would bring out a pineapple or a melon, cut into slices, and a big plateful of sugar, and we would happily dip and eat and get our faces covered with the sticky juices. At other times there were dishes of roast potatoes, left over from the luncheons, or slices of cake. Mr. Lambert owned a film projector and he often hired films and put on a film show in the tea room. We were brought up on a diet of Laurel and Hardy, Harold Lloyd, The Keystone Cops, Felix the Cat, and other stalwarts of the time, all silent with captions, and we had a wonderful time.

Sometimes in the summer Mr. Lambert took his family to Maldon, the nearest seaside town, for the day in his open topped Rover car, and if you were lucky you were sent home to ask your mother if you could go too. Holidays away from home, unless perhaps with an aunt, were unheard of in those days, so a day at the seaside was something to be talked about for a long time afterwards.

Every year, at the beginning of November, we spent days making a "guy", which would be a real work of art. This would be placed in a trolley and paraded round the village. With the money we collected from this unashamed begging we bought halfpenny bangers for Guy Fawkes Day. On the day we used these bangers to great effect, blowing up cowpats and tins, floating them down the river on pieces of bark, throwing them at girls, and generally making a nuisance of ourselves. It was always considered essential that one was put through the letterbox of the Moat House. We now know that it was a stupid and dangerous thing to do but at the time it seemed a great prank. The police were always sent for but by the time a bobby arrived on his bike we were of course somewhere else. Later in the evening the "White Horse" always had a magnificent fireworks display to which all were invited, and as soon as theirs was finished Mr. and Mrs. Rayment from the village shop lit a huge bonfire in the orchard adjoining the Trust House and put on another grand display.

The orchard had a large duck pond with a deep hole beside it which was used for filling the buckets when taking water to the chicken runs. We weren't supposed to play by the pond but we did. One day when I was playing by the pond on my own I slipped into the hole and there were a few panicky moments before I managed to claw my way out. On another occasion my brother fell into the pond and had so much mud on him that he went to the river to wash it off and told mother that he'd fallen in there.

Although we were by no means little angels and in retrospect did some quite terrible things, nothing was ever done with malice and most of our escapades were out of devilment rather than mindless vandalism. We certainly had respect for our parents and the village bobby, and if anyone was given a clip round the ear for misbehaving it was more than he dare do to tell his parents, or he would probably have got another for letting down the family. There was one occasion when we were playing cowboys and Indians on a piece of private land and suddenly one of the boys came face to face with the gamekeeper. He shouted out to us and we all ran hell for leather for about two miles, making a circuit of the village, and then calmly, we thought, strolled in from the opposite direction, firmly convinced that no-one could possibly think that we had been the culprits.

Life was so very simple in those far-off days and we made our own amusements. Sometimes we took our hoops and a short piece of stick and bowled them for miles along the country lanes. Needless to say there was very little traffic then. At other times we took a few sandwiches in a paper bag, got on our bikes, and went out for most of the day, wherever our fancy took us. Perhaps we would cycle the six miles to Hatfield to see if anything was happening at de Havilland's airfield. Or maybe we would find a wooded slope somewhere and see if we could ride from top to bottom without hitting any of the trees.

We were all great followers of cricket in those days and knew the names of all the top players and followed our favourite teams. This was the era of the cricketing greats, Len Hutton, Don Bradman, Harold Larwood, Hedley Verity, Wally Hammond, Alf Gover, C. V. Grimmet, and a host of other celebrities. We had sets of cigarette cards depicting their faces, and wearing their county caps, and we carried these around with us, making swaps in order to get a complete set. The test matches were followed closely and we were allowed to go into the lounge of the "White Horse" to listen to the commentaries on the radio. Unlike today's laid back descriptions of events the commentators described every detail of the play. "Here comes Gover running up to bowl, one, two, three, four, five, six, seven, eight, over goes his arm, slightly short, and Bradman hooks this to mid-on. Hammond races after the ball, they've taken one, two, and Hammond returns the ball to Ames. Two runs."

We played a lot of cricket over the summer months and sometimes staged our own test matches. We assumed the names of our favourite stars and played matches which sometimes took two or three days to complete. This was all very serious stuff and the rules were followed to the letter. Peter Hillyard was one of the better batsmen and soon became the regular scorer for the cricket club.

7
The River

FIXED TO THE CORNER OF THE GARAGE in the "White Horse" car park was a notice which read "Private. Footpath to rifle butts only." The path led through a small gate into the orchard next to it, past the duck pond and over a stile into the next field, a rough grassy field where horses were sometimes kept, and which led up a steep hill to the end of the White Cottages. It continued along the bottom of this field, only about one hundred yards across, then over another stile into the meadow, a large pasture field which to the left climbed a steep hill about two hundred yards long with a stand of Scots pines at the top, known locally as the plantation. On this side the field continued for about half a mile, with the Memorial Hall adjoining it about one third of the way along. Halfway down the hill, from the far end, a tongue of woodland jutted out, bisecting the field at this point. This piece of woodland was known as Chisel Shelf, owing to the fact that it formed a sharp ridge roughly in the shape of a chisel. The bottom of the field continued below this wooded ridge, bordered on the other side by the river, and must have been about a mile long at this point.

On entering the meadow at the bottom one headed for a brick-built hump-backed bridge, overhung by a very old alder tree. Just before this bridge was a very shallow part of the river, with a firm sandy bottom, which was known as the paddling pool. Here the toddlers could paddle in complete safety, as the river was no more than about eighteen inches deep at any point. About a hundred yards or so beyond the bridge, the river widened as it swung round a curve and this was the bathing pool. Some time in the past somebody had fixed up a substantially built diving board which jutted out over the shallow edge and one could dive into reasonably deep water.

A few yards away on the far side of the river, were the watercress beds, formed from a small tributary of the river and filtered through several gravel filters to ensure that the water was pure. If ever we felt thirsty we would drink from below the third filter near the watercress man's hut. The water was delicious and no-one ever had any internal problems after drinking it.

The watercress beds were a good source of sticklebacks. Set into the bed of the stream at intervals were large glazed pipes, such as are used for drains. As to why they were there we had no idea, but sticklebacks used to gather in them in shoals. The method of catching these small fish was simple - tie a piece of string around the neck of a jam jar and throw the jar into the pipe. After a few minutes pull out the jar and most times there would be several fish inside. These were carried home in triumph and kept either in jars or buckets. Needless to say the poor creatures usually died after a few days.

Further upstream was a wooden bridge and just beyond this the river disappeared among some osier beds and then into the private land belonging to Panshanger. This was the limit of our play area - officially!

Many happy hours and days were spent in and around the river, both in summer and winter alike. In the summer we set out with our towels and bathing costumes and swiftly changed among the clumps of rushes which grew in the field. Often there were jack pike lying in the pool and we threw stones to scare them away in case they bit us, but I'm sure they would have scattered at the first movement in the water. We could then dive in and swim and splash about to our hearts' content, usually until we were blue with cold. Then we would lie in the sun or run round the field to get warm and the whole process would start all over again. A great adventure was to start at the paddling pool and wade up to the bathing pool, braving the swift current under the bridge and facing the unknown perils of the bullrushes and overhanging alder trees on the way. We pretended to be explorers and were always on the lookout for crocodiles and sharks.

The biggest river adventure of all, however, was to wade downstream, past Mr. Topham's Farm on one side, and the Moat House gardens on the other, keeping low so as not to be seen, and climb out at the mill. This was considered a very daring thing to do and to us young village lads it was just the right combination of excitement and danger.

One of the village characters was Noah Copps, brother of Jim Copps the cobbler. It was said that he was the tallest man in the village sitting down, and the shortest standing up, on account of his long back and short legs. Once a year he made his way to the river for his annual bath, clutching a towel and a bar of soap. After undressing among the rushes he would walk stark naked, but with one hand strategically placed, along the diving board and do a one-handed plunge into the river. After soaping himself all over he would swim around for a short while and then, again with hand strategically placed, walk back to the rushes and, after getting dried and dressed, make his way home again until the next year.

Sometimes we went hunting for crayfish. A favourite place for these was just above the wooden bridge. Some of the boys would be in the water pulling up large clumps of weed and floating them down to the bridge where more of the boys hauled them out of the water and searched through them with a long stick. The crayfish were tangled up with the weed and they were carefully teased out and placed in a large tin can full of water. When we had a good catch they were taken back to the "White Horse" where we would light a fire and boil them till they turned red. They were then either served up as a delicacy in the dining room or perhaps sold at the Women's Institute stall.

The rifle butts were situated at the edge of the wood about fifty yards beyond the bathing pool and when firing was in progress a red flag was placed just beyond the paddling pool, which put the bathing pool out of bounds. Not to be deterred, however, we undressed by the paddling pool and then waded upstream to the bathing pool and carried on swimming as usual. The only danger we could see was if the riflemen were on the 1,000-yard range but they would still have had to fire at a 45 degree angle to put us in any peril.

The targets were situated on a flat area in front of three gravel banks dug out of the side of Chisel Shelf, which rose up steeply behind them. Three large wooden covers covered a brick-built underground chamber which was reached by means of a short flight of steps to the side. In this chamber the target carriers were situated, three metal frames on which the targets were placed, and as one was pulled down the next one rose up above the ground. After a round of firing the target was pulled down under ground and inspected. Then it was raised again and a stick with a disc on the end placed over the point of impact.

The door to the underground chamber was always kept locked, but that was no defence against determined youngsters. One day we lifted the wooden covers and one boy was brave enough to climb onto the target carrier, which immediately moved down to the bottom level. Every time he tried to climb out by means of the next carrier, the same thing happened. There were some panicky moments because if we had had to fetch someone to open the door we would all have been in serious trouble. Eventually, however, we found some large branches from the wood and lowered these down the hole and he was able to climb out. That was the only time we did that.

Another use for the butts was for catapult fights. We would line up on either side of the butts and shoot acorns at each other with no thought of the possible consequences.

Sometimes when we were enjoying a day by the river, late in the afternoon Mr. Lambert's mother, a wiry little lady known as Gran, could be seen coming across the field carrying a huge picnic basket. We would all rush to meet her and help to carry the basket to the flat area by the rifle butts. Some of us would go to the watercress beds and fill a billycan with water, someone else would light a fire, and we would have a wonderful picnic of bread and butter and raspberry jam, and large slices of fruit cake, washed down with tea made from the most delicious water in the world.

On Sundays in the summer, after morning church, our mothers sometimes sent us to fetch watercress for tea. This was a round leafed, purple coloured watercress, not often seen

The wooden bridge where we caught crayfish

The author with Trix outside Jim Copps' shop

these days, and a bunch would cost four pence. Mr. Wells, the watercress man, could usually be found, clad in rubber wading trousers, busy with a large wooden rake gently tapping out any duckweed from among the cress, or sitting in his hut splitting osier twigs. He was a real countryman with a dark, suntanned face beneath a dark beard, and wore a large battered trilby on his head. He would cut a bunch of watercress, as much as he could squeeze between the thumbs and middle fingers of both hands, and tie it into a bundle with a length of split osier. The watercress teas at the "White Horse" were legendary and were very popular among the cycling fraternity and also with the visiting cricket teams.

On the end of Chisel Shelf, about two hundred yards from the river, was a small disused gravel pit, where people used to dump rubbish such as old pots and pans and anything which wouldn't rot. There were usually wasps' nests there and a favourite game was to wander up from the river, wearing nothing but our bathing costumes, carrying a handful of large stones. Having found a wasp's nest we pelted it with stones and then ran for the river, pursued by angry wasps. If nothing else it taught us to run for I can't remember anyone ever getting stung.

One day we were playing in and around the river when a punt appeared from downstream carrying Mrs. Craig and a party of house guests. They were having difficulty propelling the punt through the weeds so half a dozen or so of us waded out to them and pushed them for about half a mile upstream until they decided they'd gone far enough. We then pushed them back again. No reward was expected for this and none was given, as after all we were only a group of urchins and they were the gentry.

One of our favourite adventure spots, especially in the winter, was a small ait near the wooden bridge which we named Formosa. To reach it one had to paddle. We were continually being told by our parents not to get our feet wet as we would "catch our death of cold", but nevertheless we used to paddle on a regular basis. We would take off our boots and socks and hang them round our necks by the laces, paddle across to the ait and, after making a thorough exploration of our tropical island, paddle back again, dry our feet on our handkerchiefs, and after a quick run round the field life and warmth soon returned to our frozen extremities.

Chisel Shelf was supposed to be out of bounds for us but we regarded it as part of our play area, especially the part near the old gravel pit. We would find old meat tins from the dump and sit on them and slide down the sloping sides of the gravel pit at a tremendous rate. The bottoms of the tins became polished to a shiny brightness and our clothes were kept clean and intact.

The river held a great fascination for me then, and still does today, with its changing patterns and swirling currents, the different green water weeds trailing out beneath the surface, the small fish darting about in the shallows and the larger ones, such as the pike, lurking in its depths, the various types of rushes and sedge and irises lining the banks, the alder trees, and the swallows sweeping low over the water in the summer catching the myriad insects hovering over the surface.

The walnut tree with "The Fobury" in the background

Hertingfordbury Park, now a nursing home

8
The Cricket Field

THE SPORTS GROUND, situated next to the churchyard, and separated from it by the drive to Mrs. Roland Smith's house, was always known as the cricket field, even though football was played on it over a longer period of the year. A field just over a hundred yards in width and perhaps a hundred and fifty yards in depth, the grass was always kept short except for the bottom fifty yards which was left rough. A five-barred gate gave access to the field in the corner nearest the church and at the far end stood the pavilion, a wooden structure with a tiled roof and creosoted sides, with a wooden verandah at the front and three white-painted panels which served as the front of the pavilion when closed, and when opened up and held in position by iron bars, became a canopy under which the scorers sat when a game was in progress.

At the rear of the pavilion was a small section where the mower and other tools were kept and the whole place had a wonderful smell of mown grass and linseed oil.

At the edge of the field on the church side stood the heavy roller, resting on its great wooden shafts which were designed to fit a horse. When this was used to level the pitch the children sat on a sort of shelf at the front of the roller to give extra weight while the men held the shafts and pulled and pushed the roller back and forth. We always had free access to the field so long as we kept off the wicket area during the cricket season.

The heavy roller was a favourite meeting place for the boys and girls of the choir as there were plenty of places to sit and after choir practice we'd congregate there for the younger boys and girls perhaps to make daisy chains or to just laze around and discuss what we were going to do next.

Work on the cricket pitch usually began on Good Friday, with gentle forking and raking to try to make good some of the damage inflicted by the footballers over the winter. We helped by fetching and carrying anything which was needed and felt very important and part of the proceedings. On Saturdays those who were keen spent the whole afternoon and evening watching the match, becoming armchair critics in the process. It was always interesting to learn where the visiting teams came from, villages with familiar names and sometimes company teams with wonderful exotic-sounding names.

We had our slogger in the team of course, one Tom Hipgrave, a strongly-built man with a swarthy face, a man of whom we were slightly afraid and treated with a great deal of respect, although he would probably have never done anybody any harm. When Tom went in to bat he was either out in a few balls or there were fireworks. When he was in form he would hit fours and sixes to the despair of the opposing bowlers. Many would sail over into the churchyard and on one memorable occasion the ball hit the church tower, about a hundred yards away.

Sometimes the ball was hit out of the ground and over the lane to the side which was bounded by an overgrown field next to the rectory. If it could not be found immediately a new ball was called for while the boys continued searching through the tangle of grass and weeds.

Then there was Bob Blanchard, brother of the team captain, who was a stonewaller. When he went in to bat we settled in for a boring spell as he methodically blocked every ball and tried to break the spirit of the bowler. Among the regular players were Bill Dolley, the slow spin bowler, Bert Gostling, known as Gander, who was the fast bowler, and Ralph George, a slightly-built man and a good all-rounder, well liked by everyone, and who was tragically killed in the war.

At the end of the drive next to the cricket field was the lodge, occupied by Mr. Bird, Mrs. Roland Smith's gardener. He was a quiet, kindly man, and would always give us a glass of water if we were thirsty. He had a Victoria plum tree which overhung the cricket field and when the plums were ripe we sometimes took the odd one thinking it would not be missed.

It was wrong, but in our children's logic we were being good by not taking many.

On the far side of the cricket field was a long field belonging to Mrs. Roland Smith which reached down to the railway line and in this field she kept a donkey. The donkey liked company and often stood by the fence to be stroked and fed sweets which it liked or bunches of grass which it usually ignored. We frequently tried to ride it but it was far too clever for that. It would either move just too far away from the fence to enable us to climb on or resolutely refuse to move if we were successful. One day during a cricket match several men from the opposing team wandered over to look at the donkey. After a while one of them, egged on by the others, climbed over the fence and managed to get seated astride him, but the donkey refused to budge. After several unsuccessful attempts to make it move the man took off his cricket cap and slapped the donkey hard on the flank with it, whereupon the donkey galloped off at a fair rate with the man waving his cap like a rodeo rider, and suddenly stopped, hurtling the rider over its head. No-one was hurt and we all had a good laugh except the unfortunate rider who was the butt of many jokes for the rest of the day.

In the winter the field was given over to football. The goalposts were erected and stayed there until the following Spring, only the nets being taken down at the end of each game. The matches were typical of a small village, with a dozen or so spectators standing at various points around the touchline and with lots of shouting going on. At half time slices of orange and lemon were handed round to the players, but some of them preferred to smoke a cigarette.

On special occasions, such as the silver jubilee of King George V and Queen Mary, or the coronation of King George VI, the field was taken over for the day and marked out with running tracks and sprint lanes. All the village took part, with races for the children such as three-legged and wheelbarrow races, 50 yard and 100 yard sprints, and 440 yard races for the young men. There were events for the parents such as egg and spoon races, and thread the needle races for married couples, where the man had to run 50 yards with a piece of cotton and thread it through the eye of a needle held by his wife at the other end of the track.

There were comic football matches between the men and women, with the men dressed in women's clothes and the women in men's clothes. There were no special rules and a great time was had by all. The day usually ended with fireworks and a dance at the Memorial Hall.

9
The Railway Station

THE RAILWAY LINE crossed St. Mary's Lane at the bottom of the hill a few hundred yards past the cricket field. The station was approached by a cul-de-sac on the far side of the bridge and was typical of small country railway stations all over England. It comprised one long building, with the ticket office at one end, the stationmaster's house in the middle, and the waiting room at the other end. The platform was long and ran beside the single track and on it stood two cast iron vending machines where one could purchase 2d bars of chocolate and Sun Maid raisins.

In the waiting room stood a weighing machine where one could obtain a ticket recording one's weight for 1d. At the end of the platform a few yards past the waiting room was a small goods siding terminating with a pair of rusty buffers.

Mr. and Mrs. Flunder lived in the station house with their two children, George and Monica. Mr. Flunder was stationmaster at one of the stations in Hertford so the house went with the job. Although George and Monica were a little younger than me, when it came to birthday parties age was irrelevant, as to gather a sufficient number to make a worthwhile party in a village meant inviting most of the children of party-going age.

Parties for George and Monica were held in the waiting room, mainly because of its size. Mrs. Flunder made delicious jellies, some containing sliced bananas or orange segments which were wonderful, and others sprinkled with desiccated coconut which I thought spoiled them as jellies are made to slip down without effort and the coconut flakes interfered with this process.

After the sandwiches, cakes, jellies, birthday cake, and

lemonade we played games such as "postman's knock". In retrospect the kisses were all so very chaste and innocent. Another game was "Nelson's eye" where objects were passed from hand to hand in the dark and one had to guess what they were. There were squeals from the girls when a peeled grape or a hard-boiled egg with its shell removed, representing Nelson's eye, was handed on.

The porter was a youngish fellow by the name of Sid Andrews, fair haired with a moustache, who wore his porter's hat at a jaunty angle and was known as "the king of the kids". There were not many trains per day through the station and apart from a few local deliveries there was not much for the porter to do and time could hang heavily for a young man. So from time to time we gathered at the station to while away the time with Sid, who had fixed up a punch bag in the goods shed where he tried to teach us the rudiments of boxing.

Sometimes during the summer months, after a train had left the station, a column of smoke would arise from the embankment a short way along the line. The tinder dry grass had been set on fire by a spark from the engine. We would break off branches of elder and run along the line to beat out the flames before they set fire to the adjoining cornfield. After a hectic fifteen or twenty minutes the fire was usually out and we returned to the station smoky and sweaty, where Sid brewed tea for us and served it in large enamel railway mugs.

On the odd occasion the farmer, having been alerted to the fact that his field was in danger, arrived to inspect the possible damage. By this time the fire was usually out and after a few minutes spent stomping around and grunting he departed without a word of thanks.

The "White Horse" was one of the places to which Sid had to deliver regularly. He loaded up the parcels on a heavy wooden trolley, which was basically just a large flat wooden platform on wheels, and steered by means of a long iron handle, with a brake which operated directly on the wheels. We helped him haul this weighty contraption up the hill to the church, where we all climbed aboard and hurtled down the hill on the other side, straight over the main road, and into the "White Horse" car park, crunching over the gravel and grinding to a skidding halt. The chances of doing that successfully in today's traffic would probably be in the region of one per cent.

One weekend we heard that filming was going to take place on the Sunday and so after church we converged on the station only to be turned away by the film crew as they did not want us mixing with their "extras". The film was "When Knights were Bold" featuring Jack Buchanan. We had the advantage over the film crew as we were on familiar ground whereas they were strangers, and we soon found a way round from the far side of the track and took up vantage points from where we could watch the proceedings with impunity.

We were surprised to see how many times an experienced actor had to do the same small part over and over again before he got it right. There were just two scenes at the station. One involved Jack Buchanan driving his sports car a few yards to the station entrance before a cheering crowd, and saying a few words to the village policeman. Once he forgot his lines, another time he caught his coat on the car door, and various other things went wrong before the director was satisfied. The other scene featured a train pulling into the station. This involved backing up along the line for a few hundred yards and steaming very slowly along to the platform. When we saw the film a few years later the train was shown steaming in like an express.

That day I was wearing a new blazer for the first time and while we were scrambling under a barbed wire fence my jacket caught on a barb, making a small triangular tear. The memory of this incident distressed me for a long time afterwards because I thought of how upset my mother must have been after having spent hard-earned money to dress me decently only to have to make repairs after just one wearing.

Where the station approach joined the lane at the bottom of the hill, a small stream passed under the lane by means of a culvert. This emerged at the side of the railway embankment for a few yards before a second, longer culvert passed diagonally under the embankment. This second culvert was very dark and curved slightly in the middle so that all that could be seen of the opening at the other end was a tiny elliptical glimmer of light. It was considered very daring to walk under both culverts, wearing Wellington boots of course, and bent almost double, emerging on the other side of the embankment and scrambling through the wire fence before we were told off for trespassing.

10
Sunday School

NOT EVERY CHILD in the village attended Sunday School but for those who did it was a rewarding experience. The school was held every Sunday afternoon in the Memorial Hall and was presided over by Mrs. Roland Smith with the assistance of her housekeeper, Miss Harrower, a Scottish lady, and the district nurse, whoever that was at the time. If the weather was exceptionally nice the class was held under the oak trees which grew in the adjoining field.

Mrs. Roland Smith was a very kind and sincere lady. Her husband held a high position in the police force and was also a lay preacher. She had four children: Granville, the elder son, of whom little was seen; Marion the elder daughter, a tall blonde lady who was a sergeant in the police force, and who occasionally took the class; Rachel, the younger daughter, who was a very quiet and lovely girl, and who died tragically after a holiday abroad; and Samuel, the younger son, a teenager at the time, and known to us as Sam. They all lived in the large house known as Hertingfordbury Park, at the end of the drive which ran between the cricket field and the church.

Sunday school was not oppressively religious and concentrated on things such as truth and honesty and of loving one's parent and friends. We sang the special types of Sunday school hymns, completely different from the church hymns, and at the end of the afternoon were all given little cards with pretty pictures on them, and carrying a text from the bible. Sometimes we were asked to make a model or a drawing depicting the text for the following week's class. A small prize would be given for the best one.

One day a man brought along a zither and we all sang along to this. Sometimes there were visits from missionaries, who talked about far distant countries, illustrated by slides from a magic lantern. These meetings were usually, but not always, held at the house, as were many other extramural activities. On such an occasion we walked down the long drive in groups of two or three and presented ourselves at the front door. Miss Harrower would welcome us and take us to the large drawing room, where the magic lantern, a magnificent piece of equipment made from brass and polished wood, would be standing on a large wooden tripod in the centre of the room. There were often costumes from the country concerned, and suitably sized children were dressed in these before the talk began.

To see the wonderful pictures of places such as India, China, Tibet, etc., filled us with wonder, and no-one in those far-off days thought that perhaps at some time in the future many of us would visit these countries either as a member of one of the services, for business, or just taking a holiday. A missionary who had spent many years in China brought two young Chinese girls with her. One of them, a slim little girl, spoke perfect English, taught by the missionaries, while the other was a tiny Chinese princess who had been cast out onto the streets by her parents because she was deaf and dumb. The missionaries had taken her into their care and it was evident from the happy smiles depicted on the slides that they had given her a quality of life which otherwise she could never have known.

Every year there was an Easter egg hunt in the grounds of the house. On arrival we were each given a piece of paper with a number on it and we then had to search all round the large garden to find another piece of paper with a corresponding number. When we had both pieces of paper we took them back to the house and received an Easter egg with the same number on it. If there were any numbers left over we could then go and look for another one. There were excited cries of "have you seen this number" as we searched through the clumps of pampas grass and among the trees and shrubs. Sometimes the eggs were chocolate eggs and sometimes they were made of cardboard with sweets and a packet of nasturtium seeds inside. Whether or not the number was found no-one went home empty-handed and it was a wonderful morning out.

At other times some of the older children went to the house in the evenings and made things for the annual sale of work. The girls sewed cushion covers and table runners while the boys made bath salts. There would be a large tub full of soda crystals and various jars of coloured and scented water. The liquid was poured over the crystals and stirred round by hand until the crystals had absorbed all the water and then they were placed in jars ready for sale. We also used to knit pairs of braces although I can't imagine them being of any use.

Sometimes the whole class was taken on an outing. One very memorable one was a trip to London to see the Walt Disney film "Snow White and the Seven Dwarfs". We went to London by train, had lunch at Lyon's Corner House and then went to the New Gallery Cinema, Regent Street, to see the film. I remember we were all given a foul-tasting lozenge to suck in the cinema to combat the "London germs".

Another outing was to Regent's Park Zoo. We travelled up by means of several cars, our car being driven by Mrs. Maitland, a diminutive lady who raced cars at Brooklands Park racing circuit. Traffic was fairly light in those days and as we were approaching London on the Great Cambridge Road we could see a motor cycle in the distance. Mrs. Maitland asked us if we'd like to overtake it and of course we said "yes". With that she put her toe down hard on the accelerator and we shot past the astonished motor cyclist at 85 m.p.h. This was absolute magic and was talked about for days afterwards.

This particular outing holds very special memories for me. On the way home I started to get abdominal pains which gradually worsened and by the time I reached home I could not stand upright. The pain became severe in the evening and the doctor was sent for. He diagnosed appendicitis and sent for the ambulance. The memory of the next few hours is a blurred one of street lights flashing by the ambulance windows, overhead lights in the hospital corridors, prodding by a grave-faced surgeon, followed by pre-operative procedures, and being wheeled to the operating theatre.

There a large steel mask padded with cotton wool was

placed over my face, ether was dripped on to it, the anaesthetist was talking to me and I was struggling to answer, there was a sensation of going up in a lift, and then, suddenly, oblivion.

I came to with a nurse holding me gently but firmly to prevent a drip tube in my arm from being pulled out. I later discovered I had had an internal abscess. I spent five weeks in hospital and remember with affection the caring nurses, my family visits, and the concern felt by many of my friends and fellow villagers.

When I was home once more and on the road to recovery Mrs. Leslie paid for me to go for three weeks to a convalescent home at Hunstanton to which she subscribed, and Mrs. Roland Smith and her family paid many supportive visits.

The three weeks I spent at Hunstanton was a totally new experience for me. It was the first seaside holiday I'd ever had and it was all the more memorable because it was hot and sunny all the time I was there. Sleeping in a dormitory with other men and boys and eating in a communal hall were completely new to me but I quickly became accustomed to the routine and as my strength returned I had a wonderful time.

However, war clouds were gathering. There was a practice air raid alert during my stay and although it didn't mean much to me at the time only a few months were to elapse before it became a grim reality.

I returned home from convalescence to find new faces in the village, children with unfamiliar accents. The first evacuees had arrived.

11
The End of Childhood

AS WE NEARED PUBERTY subtle changes took place in our lives. We lost interest in children's games and looked for more manly things to do. One of the favourite pastimes in the summer was to go to the harvest field and help bring in the corn. The dusty smell of freshly cut corn on a warm summer day is difficult to describe but it acted like a magnet to us. Cutting was done with a horse-drawn binder, a dangerous-looking contraption with huge blades criss-crossing in front of a rotating canvas sheet which took the loose corn into the interior of the binder. A sheaf of corn would emerge from the other side, neatly tied with a length of binder string, and be dumped unceremoniously on the ground. We then gathered these up two at a time and brought them together with about six more to form a stook.

As more and more of the corn was cut and the area of standing corn became smaller, men, some armed with shot-guns and a few with catapults, gathered round the perimeter to shoot the rabbits and rats as they ran out to escape the jaws of the binder. We watched fascinated as the shot rabbits were given a sharp rap on the back of the neck with the edge of the hand to ensure they were dead, and stretched and gutted on the spot. It all seems barbaric now but in those days it was a country way of life and rabbit was an essential part of a countryman's diet.

At the age of twelve we were allowed to go beating for partridges and pheasants. To become a beater it was necessary to be a friend of one of the boys whose uncle was the head gamekeeper and who recruited the requisite number. Having been accepted into this rather elite little band the first thing to do was to cut oneself a good stout hazel stick which served both to rattle the stones and trees so as to frighten up the game and to beat down the nettles and brambles which impeded our progress.

Partridge shooting began in September and we sometimes had to walk two or three miles to the starting point. We then lined up across a field well spaced out from each other. The head keeper blew his hunting horn and we walked across the fields tapping our sticks on the ground and driving the birds towards the guns. Spaced out between us were the gamekeepers with their dogs who retrieved any birds which fell between the line of beaters and the shooters. One of the keepers, Ted Carter, a lean, florid faced man, would shout at us to keep in line, using language we had never heard before and which was seldom used even between working men. Occasionally we walked across mushroom fields and would stop to pick these, which brought forth more swearing from Ted Carter, but we didn't mind this too much as we could sell these to the shooters, who mostly came from London and consequently valued fresh mushrooms.

We probably walked about eight to ten miles during the course of the day and after the shoot was over we then had to walk home, so we may have covered some twelve to fourteen miles in all. For this we earned three shillings and sixpence and a bottle of ginger beer to drink with our sandwiches at lunchtime. The men received ten shillings and a bottle of beer.

One day the first field we had to walk through included a large patch of kale. It had rained the previous night and the curly leaves of the kale were full of large droplets of water. Those of us who had to walk through this were soaked from the waist downwards and remained wet for the rest of the day. As it happened the last drive of the day took in another field of kale. The head keeper asked which of the boys had walked through the kale in the morning. Naturally those of us who had done so spoke up. "Well," he said, "you're wet already so you can go through again!"

Later in the year pheasant shooting began which was much more fun as it involved walking through woods and thickets, rattling the trees with our sticks. Sometimes some of the boys were put "on stop" which meant going with one of the keepers to some distant point and waiting there, perhaps for half a day or maybe longer, and drive any birds which emerged back into the woods. To most of us this meant an opportunity for a quiet read, and in anticipation of this we would take one of the boys' magazines with us, discreetly tucked into an inside pocket.

On one such occasion a small group of us were taken with one of the older gamekeepers to a point where the shoot would finish at the end of the day. It was a really cold day and the keeper said there was no point in our standing at the edge of the wood all day so we should light a fire and make ourselves comfortable for a few hours. This was where our boy scout training came in useful. Using tufts of dried grass and tiny scraps of dry bark and twigs we soon had a small fire going. This was gradually added to until eventually we were bringing in large branches and by lunchtime had a roaring bonfire going around which we all sat and enjoyed our sandwiches and ginger beer till late in the afternoon when we heard the sound of the approaching beaters. The fire was then hastily smothered and we took up our positions at the edge of the wood as though we had been there all day.

The threat of war brought a distinct change to the atmosphere of the village so far as the children were concerned. It was something we didn't quite comprehend and there was an air of excitement, especially among the boys. We had previously had lessons at school about Adolf Hitler and his annexing of various countries, and in 1938 a young Jewish girl, Eva Bauer, a refugee from Germany, joined our class, but we had no idea of the scale of things or of the horrors of war. There was no television to give on-the-spot coverage of events, only disembodied radio reports. The older men talked with grave faces about what it was like in the "last war" but to the rest of us whom war had never touched it was something which happened far away and the pain and terror could not even begin to be imagined.

The school became a distribution centre for gas masks where we were instructed how to use them and the older children had to take them round to all the houses in Hertingfordbury and the Greens and make certain that everybody had one and knew how to use it.

We had to dig trenches in the field next to the school playground in case of air raids with the help of one or two men. The soil was clay and after the first rains of the winter they filled with water which soon became stagnant and they were eventually filled in as they were more of a potential hazard than the raids themselves. A similar thing happened in the village. Trenches were dug in the plantation, this time in sandy soil. In spite of being shored up with planks of wood the sides of the trenches kept collapsing and they were never used. Sir Henry Richards was appointed Chief Warden of the A.R.P., later to be called Civil Defence, and Dell Cottage became the warden's post.

In 1939, however, when war was declared, things changed rapidly. Windows were criss-crossed with sticky paper to prevent flying glass in the event of bombing and thick dark curtains were hung at windows or wooden frames covered with brown paper were made to place in the windows at night to prevent chinks of light. Young men began to disappear from the village as they were called up for one or other of the armed forces. Barrage balloons could be seen glinting in the sunlight in the direction of London, only about twenty miles away, and air raid warnings began to interrupt the routine of village life, by both day and night. We used to sit in the fields watching the squadrons of bombers flying towards London, tiny silver things high in the sky, with even smaller fighters weaving in and out. Occasionally one would fall away but it seemed so remote and something apart from our lives. We would buy model aeroplane kits and make up both English and German aeroplanes and hang them up on a clothes line and stage dogfights.

Convoys of army trucks trundled through the village and we lined the streets to watch them and wave to the soldiers. Sometimes they set up camp in one of the fields on the perimeter of the village and stayed there for a few days and some of the older girls would hang around making eyes at the men.

Posters were distributed showing how to deal with German paratroopers, a futile gesture but it served to keep up morale.

Meantime we boys were busy making anti-personnel bombs from screwtop bottles partly filled with water and carbide. These were lethal, throwing shards of glass as far as a hundred yards when they exploded, and we really thought we would be some sort of resistance movement if the Germans actually invaded.

One day a German bomber was shot down just outside the village. We cycled up to see it the following day and were surprised to discover how small it seemed. The crew had survived unhurt and were taken prisoner.

It was in 1939 that the new Education Act came into force. All children over the age of eleven had to go to a secondary modern school, which meant travelling to Hertford on the school bus every day. The girls went to Port Vale School and the boys to Longmores School. The village school became an infants and junior school and Mr. Rayment left to become a school inspector in Newcastle-upon-Tyne.

Evacuees from London were billeted in the village, among them boys from the Battersea Grammar School, wearing their distinctive black and white striped jackets. The school, which was moved in its entirety to Hertford, boasted a magnificent school band, which was very popular at parades and could often be seen preceding their army cadet force on a march through the town.

The Rector, the Reverend Bond, joined the army as a padre and was replaced by a Reverend Mackenzie who started a scout troop, assisted by Harold Blanchard, the church warden. We met in the "White Horse" tea room and had a great time learning knots, first aid, basic cooking and self-preservation, and played the wonderful game of British Bulldogs, which is something between a rugger scrum and a lynching.

We went out with the trek cart collecting waste paper for the war effort, and in the autumn took carrier bags and sacks across the fields and along the hedgerows to gather rose hips. This was done in association with the Girl Guides, the first time that most of us had had any experience of working in co-operation with girls. We were growing up.

A number of us started work the year after the war started as school leaving age was then fourteen. We were no longer free spirits and looked forward to the evenings, and especially to the weekends, when the time from Saturday noon till eight o'clock on Monday morning was our own. We were now earning money and although most of it was given to our parents there was enough left over to go the cinema once a week and if we walked there and back there would be a few pence left over for sweets.

A youth club was formed in the early years of the war and we met weekly in the schoolroom in the evenings, where there were board and card games, dancing, and boxing lessons for the boys. One winter evening Miss Daniels, the head teacher and youth club leader, informed us that the air raids were getting closer and we ought to go home immediately. We went outside and the woods just two fields away were ablaze with incendiary bombs and the sky in the direction of London was glowing a deep red and peppered with the starry bursts of anti-aircraft fire. We formed up into threes and fours and did the Palais Glide all the way home down the middle of the road, completely oblivious to the danger and to the concern of our parents.

Soon, however, the realities of war began to make themselves known. In Hertingfordbury itself a V2 rocket fell in a field just beyond the wardens' post, two five-hundred pound bombs fell in the garden of Dell Cottage, six smaller bombs fell in the kitchen gardens of Epcombs, an oil bomb landed in the churchyard, and a stick of incendiary bombs fell on the railway line and rectory, starting numerous small fires but fortunately without causing casualties.

Half a mile from Hertingfordbury was the small hamlet of Staines Green where my aunt's cottage stood by the road side bounded on three sides by fields. Three five-hundred pound bombs fell in line with the cottage in the field to the left, six small bombs fell in the paddock at the rear, and a one thousand pounder fell in the field on the right hand side of the cottage, and not even a window pane was broken.

As the war dragged on more and more of the lads were called up for military service, and those not yet old enough joined the Civil Defence or the Air Training Corps. The days of childhood and innocence had passed.

Books Published by THE BOOK CASTLE

COUNTRYSIDE CYCLING IN BEDFORDSHIRE, BUCKINGHAMSHIRE AND HERTFORDSHIRE: Mick Payne.
Twenty rides on- and off-road for all the family.

PUB WALKS FROM COUNTRY STATIONS:
Bedfordshire and Hertfordshire: Clive Higgs.
Fourteen circular country rambles, each starting and finishing at a railway station and incorporating a pub-stop at a mid-way point.

PUB WALKS FROM COUNTRY STATIONS:
Buckinghamshire and Oxfordshire: Clive Higgs.
A further selection of unusual rural rambles.

LOCAL WALKS: South Bedfordshire and North Chilterns:
Vaughan Basham.
Twenty-seven thematic circular walks.

LOCAL WALKS: North and Mid Bedfordshire: Vaughan Basham.
Twenty-five thematic circular walks.

FAMILY WALKS: Chilterns South: Nick Moon.
Thirty 3 to 5 mile circular walks.

FAMILY WALKS: Chilterns North: Nick Moon.
Thirty further shortish country walks.

CHILTERN WALKS: Hertfordshire, Bedfordshire and North Buckinghamshire: Nick Moon.
CHILTERN WALKS: Buckinghamshire: Nick Moon.
CHILTERN WALKS: Oxfordshire and West Buckinghamshire: Nick Moon.
A trilogy of circular walks, in association with the Chiltern Society. Each volume contains 30 circular walks.

OXFORDSHIRE WALKS:
Oxford, the Cotswolds and the Cherwell Valley: Nick Moon.
OXFORDSHIRE WALKS:
Oxford, the Downs and the Thames Valley: Nick Moon.
Two volumes that complement Chiltern Walks: Oxfordshire and complete coverage of the county, in association with the Oxford Fieldpaths Society. Thirty circular walks in each.

JOURNEYS INTO BEDFORDSHIRE: Anthony Mackay.
Foreword by The Marquess of Tavistock, Woburn Abbey. A lavish book of over 150 evocative ink drawings.

MANORS and MAYHEM, PAUPERS and PARSONS: Tales from Four Shire: Beds., Bucks., Herts., and Northants.: John Houghton
Little-known historical snippets and stories.

MYTHS and WITCHES, PEOPLE and POLITICS: Tales from Four Shires: Bucks., Beds., Herts., and Northants.: John Houghton.
Anthology of strange, but true historical events.

HISTORIC FIGURES IN THE BUCKINGHAMSHIRE LANDSCAPE: John Houghton.
Major personalities and events that have shaped the county's past, including a special section on Bletchley Park.

FOLK: Characters and Events in the History of Bedfordshire and Northamptonshire: Vivienne Evans.
Anthology about people of yesteryear – arranged alphabetically by village or town.

BEDFORDSHIRE'S YESTERYEARS Vol 2:
The Rural Scene: Brenda Fraser Newstead.
Vivid first-hand accounts of country life two or three generations ago.

BEDFORDSHIRE'S YESTERYEARS Vol 3:
Craftsmen and Tradespeople: Brenda Fraser Newstead.
Fascinating recollections over several generations practising many vanishing crafts and trades.

BEDFORDSHIRE'S YESTERYEARS Vol 4:
Wat Times and Civil Matters: Brenda Fraser Newstead.
Two World Wars, plus transport, law and order, etc.

THE RAILWAY AGE IN BEDFORDSHIRE: Fred Cockman.
Classic, illustrated account of early railway history.

GLEANINGS REVISITED:
Nostalgic Thoughts of a Bedfordshire Farmer's Boy:
E W O'Dell.
His own sketches and early photographs adorn this lively account of rural Bedfordshire in days gone by.

FARM OF MY CHILDHOOD, 1925–1947: Mary Roberts.
An almost vanished lifestyle on a remote farm near Flitwick.

SWANS IN MY KITCHEN: Lis Dorer.
Story of a Swan Sanctuary near Hemel Hempstead.

DUNSTABLE WITH THE PRIORY: 1100–1550: Vivienne Evans.
Dramatic growth of Henry I's important new town around a major crossroads.

DUNSTABLE DECADE: THE EIGHTIES:
A Collection of Photographs: Pat Lovering.
A souvenir book of 300 pictures of people and events in the 1980s.

DUNSTABLE IN DETAIL: Nigel Benson.
A hundred of the town's buildings and features, plus town trail map.

OLD DUNSTABLE: Bill Twaddle.
A new edition of this collection of early photographs.

BOURNE and BRED: A Dunstable Boyhood Between the Wars:
Colin Bourne.
An elegantly written, well-illustrated book capturing the spirit of the town over fifty years ago.

ROYAL HOUGHTON: Pat Lovering:
Illustrated history of Houghton Regis from the earliest times to the present.

THE CHANGING FACE OF LUTON: An Illustrated History:
Stephen Bunker, Robin Holgate and Marian Nichols.
Luton's development from earliest times to the present busy industrial town. Illustrated in colour and monochrome

THE MEN WHO WORE STRAW HELMETS:
Policing Luton, 1840–1974: Tom Madigan.
Meticulously chronicled history; dozens of rare photographs; author served in Luton Police for fifty years.

BETWEEN THE HILLS: The Story of Lilley, a Chiltern Village:
Roy Pinnock.
A priceless piece of our heritage – the rural beauty remains but the customs and way of life described here have largely disappeared.

A HATTER GOES MAD!: Kristina Howells.
Luton Town footballers, officials and supporters talk to a female fan.

LEGACIES: Tales and Legends of Luton and the North Chilterns:
Vic Lea.
Twenty-five mysteries and stories based on fact, including Luton Town Football Club. Many photographs.

LEAFING THROUGH LITERATURE:
Writers' Lives in Hertfordshire and Bedfordshire: David Carroll.
Illustrated short biographies of many famous authors and their connections with these counties.

A PILGRIMAGE IN HERTFORDSHIRE: H M Alderman.
Classic, between-the-wars tour round the county, embellished with line drawings.

CHILTERN ARCHAEOLOGY: RECENT WORK:
A Handbook for the Next Decade: edited by Robin Holgate.
The latest views, results and excavations by twenty-three leading archaeologists throughout the Chilterns.

THE HILL OF THE MARTYR:
An Architectural History of St. Albans Abbey: Eileen Roberts.
Scholarly and readable chronological narrative history of Hertfordshire and Bedfordshire's famous cathedral. Fully illustrated with photographs and plans.

THE TALL HITCHIN SERGEANT:
A Victorian Crime Novel Based on Fact: Edgar Newman.
Mixes real police officers and authentic background with an exciting storyline.

THE TALL HITCHIN INSPECTOR'S CASEBOOK:
A Victorian Crime Novel Based on Fact: Edgar Newman.
Worthies of the time encounter more archetypal villains.

SPECIALLY FOR CHILDREN

VILLA BELOW THE KNOLLS: A Story of Roman Britain:
Michael Dundrow.
An exciting adventure for young John in Totternhoe and Dunstable two thousand years ago.

THE RAVENS: One Boy Against the Might of Rome:
James Dyer.
On the Barton Hills and in the south-east of England as the men of the great fort of Ravensburgh (near Hexton) confront the invaders.

Further titles are in preparation.
All the above are available via any bookshop, or from the publisher and bookseller

THE BOOK CASTLE
12 Church Street, Dunstable Bedfordshire, LU5 4RU
Tel: (01582) 605670